WASHINGTON
STATE
A Photographic Journey

TEXT: **Bill Harris**

CAPTIONS: **Fleur Robertson**

DESIGNED BY: **Teddy Hartshorn**

EDITORIAL: **Gill Waugh**

PRODUCTION: **Ruth Arthur and David Proffit**

DIRECTOR OF PRODUCTION: **Gerald Hughes**

CLB 2673
© 1991 Colour Library Books Ltd., Godalming, Surrey, England.
All rights reserved.
This 1991 edition published by Crescent Books,
distributed by Outlet Book Company, Inc., a Random House Company,
225 Park Avenue South, New York, New York 10003.
Color separations by Tien Wah Press (PTE) Ltd.
Printed and bound in Singapore.
ISBN 0 517 06028 0
8 7 6 5 4 3 2 1

WASHINGTON
STATE
A Photographic Journey

Text by
BILL HARRIS

CRESCENT BOOKS
NEW YORK

More than thirty years before Captain John Smith sailed up the northeastern coast of North America and named it New England, Sir Francis Drake had sailed past the opposite coast and, possibly because it was raining that day, his thoughts turned to home and he called it Nova Albion, which means the same thing. Some 250 years later, after New Englanders had taken to calling themselves Americans, it was still undecided as to whether the Pacific Northwest above the Columbia River would become a part of the United States or always be an outpost of the British Empire.

The British didn't pay a lot of attention to the Northwest until 1776, when events in the Northeast made them think it might be a good idea to get serious about finding the Northwest Passage across the continent before the American rebels claimed all of it. They sent Captain James Cook who, after a sojourn in Hawaii, which he discovered on the way, arrived at the coast of North America in 1778 and claimed it all for the same King George III who was losing his toehold back East. Cook's men also discovered sea otters in the waters off the Northwest, and before they finished their voyage they discovered that the Chinese were willing to pay plenty for more of them. It brought the English back in search of more furs. Meanwhile, the Spanish were already there but, before long, thanks to events on the other side of the world, they decided to concentrate on California instead of the lands further north. It left the British, in the person of Captain George Vancouver, free to claim not only the coast, but the interior, too.

It wasn't as though the Americans hadn't been active there. Captain Robert Gray discovered and explored the mouth of the Columbia River in 1792. He named it in honor of his ship, the first American vessel to sail around the world. But Vancouver's men took the much shorter voyage up the river and decided it was theirs in spite of Gray's accomplishments. John Jacob Astor established a fur trading post, which he modestly named Astoria, at the mouth of the Columbia in 1811, but a year later, the British-controlled North West Company took it over. The treaty that ended the War of 1812 gave the former combatants joint custody of the territory south of 54 degrees, 40 minutes north latitude, above which, both the Americans and the British agreed, was Russian territory.

Several American parties explored the Pacific Northwest during the years of joint occupation, and in spite of a wave of Anglophobia that was sweeping the United States east of the Mississippi at the time, the representatives of both England and America got along surprisingly well. But there was no mistake who was in charge. It was neither the British nor the Americans. It was the Hudson's Bay Company.

By the mid-1820s, the Bay had absorbed the old North West Company and had also managed to eliminate all the other competition in the fur business. Among the trading posts it acquired in the merger with North West was the former American fort at Astoria, which it moved to the north bank of the Columbia River because it seemed certain that the day wasn't far off when the Oregon Territory south of the river would become American. But no one on either side of the river had any doubt that the Union Jack would fly forever north of the Columbia. Before long the English moved about a hundred miles up the river, and concentrated their operations in a new fort they named for George Vancouver, who had taken their flag there in the first place.

Fort Vancouver became the business and social center of the entire Northwest under the tough but benevolent hand of the company's chief factor, Dr. John McLaughlin. When the Hudson's Bay Company first moved into the territory, its frugal directors back in London were appalled to discover that its predecessors had an inordinate taste for the good life, even in their wild surroundings. When they received past due bills for salmon that had been imported from Scotland, they put their foot down and decreed that their trading posts were to be self-supporting. Salmon was no problem, but the men who ran the posts were trappers and fur traders, not farmers. They were also company men, though, and before long they were planting orchards and establishing farms and cattle ranches. Their efforts not only saved the company money, but added new profit centers at the same time. They also made the Oregon Territory more attractive to settlers, who were impressed by the richness of the land. The problem was that the newcomers weren't coming from England, but from America. By 1843, there were more Americans in the Northwest than all the other nationalities combined, and settlers in the Willamette Valley and along the lower Columbia had already formed their own government, although the area wouldn't be given official Territorial status for another five years.

Meanwhile, there was strong agitation back East to drive the British out. The Bay Company had already moved its headquarters up to Fort Victoria on Vancouver Island, but new American arrivals still concentrated their search for new homesites south of the Columbia, because they weren't convinced the British wouldn't be coming back. Others who dreamed of following them wanted reassurance that they wouldn't find themselves in a British colony, and in 1844 they cast their presidential votes for James K. Polk in response to his campaign slogan "Fifty-four-forty or fight!" As it turned out, as president, Polk turned his clenched fist much further south and went to war with Mexico over Texas rather than with England over Oregon, and when it was all over he had added the Southwest rather than the Northwest to the territory of the United States. Britain was in no mood for a fight anyway, and compromised with the Polk Administration to set the Oregon Territory's boundary at the 49th parallel. Congress approved the treaty in 1848, and five years later Oregon was divided in two, with the area above the Columbia River called Washington. Its original name was to be Columbia, but Senator Stanton of Kentucky suggested it would be nice to name it Washington in honor of the first president. Some of his colleagues were worried that the name would cause endless confusion between the Territory, which they knew would eventually become a state, and the National Capital. But their objections were hooted down. Though today's Washingtonians are perfectly happy with their state's name, many of them have to admit that the Congressmen were probably right, because they are forced to waste a lot of energy explaining that they live in the state of, not the city of, Washington. On the other hand, if cooler heads had prevailed in favor of naming it Columbia, they'd probably spend just as much time explaining the difference between the state of and the District of Columbia.

The original Washington Territory included all of the present state, the northern part of Idaho and the western part of Montana. When its status became official, the 193,000-square-mile Territory's population, not counting Indians, was 3,965. Thirty-six years later, in 1889, when it became the 42d of the United States, its boundaries had shifted several times, and though it was smaller its population had grown to 173,181. The number probably should have been higher, but the Territory had been plagued by an unusual problem. Through most of its early years, ninety percent of all Washingtonians were men.

Among those men was Asa Mercer, who crossed the country in a wagon train in 1861. Not long after he arrived, either because he was a recent college graduate or in spite of it, he got a job clearing land for the new Territorial University. Then he was asked to help raise the building, and when it was finished he had become such a fixture around the place that he was made the institution's first president and its only teacher. The job gave him a certain amount of status even if the pay was poor, and young Asa became involved in community affairs. It was obviously the only kind of affair any man could involve himself in back then, but Mercer set out to use his new-found influence to help change all that.

He was able to convince the territorial governor that Washington's salvation was tied to getting more women there, and then he went on to the legislature with a plan to send him east to recruit some. Others before him had advertised for female settlers but the cost of transporting individuals across the country made it impossible for any of them to start a trend. Mercer argued that if they were brought in large numbers, say five hundred at a time, the per capita cost would be relatively low. The legislature agreed and gave him its blessing. But it didn't have any money to give him. That was no problem for Asa Mercer, though. He went from door to door begging for funds, and before long he had the price of a ticket to Boston. And why not? Few men in the history of the world have ever suggested a more appealing crusade.

The idea was appealing to the ladies back east, too. Hundreds of women had been widowed by the Civil War; hundreds more had been thrown out of work by the slowdown in the New England textile mills, with no prospect of finding a husband, and going west seemed like the answer to a maiden's prayer. In a matter of weeks Mercer had more than enough candidates, but by the time the ship was ready to sail, most of them got cold feet and he was forced to go home with only eleven female companions. When he pulled into Seattle with his charges, they were seasick and he was discouraged, but every man – and woman – in the Territory regarded Asa Mercer as a genuine hero. They were so grateful that they elected him to the legislature. No one was more surprised than he was. "I never had to buy a cigar or a glass of whiskey for anybody," he said.

About a year and a half later, he decided to try again. Abraham Lincoln was in the White House and Mercer felt that if he could arrange to meet the president and get his blessing, he wouldn't have any problem at all. But when he arrived in New York on his way to Washington, he found the city in mourning. President Lincoln had been assassinated the previous evening. Undaunted, Mercer went on to the capital and buttonholed everyone he could, from President Andrew Johnson on down. They all agreed with his philosophy that "all the goodness in the world comes from the influence of pure-minded women." But, possibly because women couldn't vote in those days, none of the elected officials was willing to commit any funds to the scheme.

It wasn't a total loss, though. General Ulysses S. Grant, who had seen service in the Oregon Territory before the war and knew firsthand what Mercer was talking about, persuaded the president to commit a war surplus steamboat to the project. But after Mercer went to New York to round up applicants, the Army quartermaster refused to honor the request, claiming it was illegal. Then, as the women were unpacking their bags, the quartermaster made a counteroffer. He wasn't prepared to give a ship away, but he was willing to sell one. But his asking price of $80,000, though a real bargain, was too rich for Mercer's blood. He didn't even have the price of a ticket to get himself back home. Then fate stepped in.

A steamship operator named Ben Holladay heard of the quartermaster's offer and smelled an opportunity to get himself a new ship for about a third of its cost. He approached Mercer and offered to give him the price of the boat and then to transport five hundred women to Seattle at a special reduced fare in exchange for the vessel when the voyage was over. Mercer was overjoyed and they were practically on their way. Or so he thought.

Naturally, all this activity produced a lot of publicity, and Americans who read about Asa Mercer over their morning coffee weren't sure whether they should be amused, supportive or shocked. Just before the ship was set to sail, the newspapers made up their mind for them. The *New York Herald* started the ball rolling with a front page story charging that the women Mercer had recruited were destined for Seattle brothels, and they backed up the story with sidebars on the rough and tumble life of the men who lived on the shores of Puget Sound. Other papers added lurid embellishments, and almost overnight two hundred of the Mercer Girls cancelled their contracts. Then Ben Holladay produced his contract.

He pointed out that the special fare was based on carrying five hundred passengers and that he'd have to charge full fare for a lesser number. No matter that he had saved $160,000 on the cost of a steamship. Mercer wasn't in any position to argue such fine points. The ship finally sailed from New York on January 6, 1866 and arrived in San Francisco ninety-six days later. By then Mercer's fame had preceded him, and they were met at the Golden Gate by thousands of men bent on persuading the women to go no further. Then the captain of the ship revealed that he wasn't going any further anyway. Apparently Ben Holladay had planned it that way all along, because it was easier to recruit passengers for the return trip from San Francisco. There were even some uncharitable souls who said that he had planted those newspaper stories, too, so that the outward voyage would be more profitable. Be that as it may, they read newspapers in Seattle, too, and the men there, though pleased to see the women who limped into town on some lumber ships headed back for a fresh cargo, blamed Mercer for giving them a bad reputation. Within a few months all the girls were married, one of them even became Asa Mercer's bride. But Mr. Mercer was a pariah in his adopted hometown and eventually drifted into Oregon, then inland to Wyoming and south to Arizona. But his luck never changed.

Washington's luck began to change at about the same time the Mercer Girls arrived, but the women had little more to do with it than than Asa Mercer had been responsible for giving the Territory a bad name. Congress had ratified treaties with the Indians a half dozen years before, and by the time the ladies began settling down, the formerly hostile tribes were being resettled on new reservations. It was the end of an Indian war that made most of the others seem positively tame and had made prospective settlers think twice about moving into the Northwest.

Most of the people who migrated there went across the country on the Oregon Trail. Some 300,000 went in the 1840s and '50s, and though about two-thirds of them were headed for the California gold fields, enough opted to head north to make a difference. The stories of their travails along the way have become the stuff of the American legend, but though most of the tales of hardship are quite true, one aspect that has been exaggerated is the Indian menace. In twenty years, more than 10,000 pioneers wound up along the trail in shallow graves, but of that number less than 400 were killed by Indians. In fact, many wagon train emigrants never saw a red man in the twenty weeks it took to travel the 1,900 miles from the Missouri River to the Columbia River Valley. It wasn't until they got there that the Indians became a problem.

The earliest white men to land in the Northwest found the natives generally hostile, but as traders began arriving they found them enthusiastic business partners, and for a half century or so the races lived in relative peace, with the red men showing the whites how to survive in the new country. Missionaries who began arriving in the early years of the nineteenth century were bent on returning the favor by saving Indian souls and setting them on the right path toward the Great Beyond. But it turned out to be a bumpy road. The Congregationalist American Board of Commissioners for Foreign Missions, which had such great success with the heathen in Hawaii, sent one of its best men, the Reverend Jonathan S. Green, on a scouting mission into the Oregon Territory in 1827, and though his report was pessimistic, it encouraged other Congregationalists to take up the challenge. But the Methodists beat them to it when Jason Lee and his nephew, Daniel, a minister of the church, established a mission that grew to a string of six. The Indians largely ignored them, but they made the Territory respectable enough to encourage more Americans to move there. The foreign mission commissioners were encouraged, too, and in 1836 they sent a group headed by Dr. Marcus Whitman, a Presbyterian, to see if Reverend Green might have been a bit hasty in his judgement. He concluded that the fur traders and mountain men needed to get religion just as much as the Indians, and went home to upstate New York to organize a party dedicated to the two-fold quest of ministering to backsliding whites as well as to the savages.

The commissioners had a strong rule that its missionaries should be married couples. The fact that Whitman was single made him a controversial choice, but they bent the rule because he was a medical doctor. But Marcus Whitman wasn't going to be single for long. Back home in Western New York there lived a girl named Narcissa Prentiss, a devout Presbyterian with the zeal of a missionary. She longed to save the heathen, but at the age of twenty-six she still hadn't found a suitable husband, and it was considered impossible for a spinster to answer God's call, no matter how loudly she heard it. Then one day, out of the blue, Dr. Whitman appeared at her door. She hardly knew him, but she was impressed by his pious ways, and when he asked her point-blank to marry him and go along with him to deliver the Word of God to the Indians, she accepted without giving it a second thought. A few months later, Narcissa and her new husband were on a wagon train headed west.

There was no question that Dr. Whitman had made the right choice. Narcissa was a lovely young woman, the cultured daughter of a respected judge, light-haired and blue-eyed and bubbling over with genuine enthusiasm tempered with quiet charm. As they crossed the Rockies she created a gentle stir at a rendezvous of mountain men, and by the time they arrived at Fort Vancouver word had spread that this was no ordinary woman. Every settlement in the Territory competed for the honor of having the Whitmans live among them, but the Doctor opted to move into the wilderness, establishing his mission about two dozen miles from the Columbia in the Walla Walla Valley, at a place the Cayuse Indians called *Waiilatpu*.

Mrs. Whitman was one of the first two white women to cross the plains. The other was Eliza Spalding, the bride of Reverend Henry Spalding, a woman a future generation would characterize as a "pill." Her constant complaining was a marked contrast to Narcissa's enthusiasm, but there was another, more important reason why they couldn't get along with each other. Reverend Spalding had grown up with Narcissa and always assumed she would become his wife. When she told him she'd prefer spinsterhood to life at his side, he never forgave her. It was obvious that the Whitmans and the Spaldings could never work together to dispense Christian charity, and after a few tense weeks at Waiilatpu, the minister and his wife went off to set up their own mission in the Snake River country well out of earshot.

There was still a problem, though. Whitman was a doctor, not a minister, and if both he and his wife had strong religious convictions, neither of them had the training to be evangelists. They established a church anyway, and though they didn't understand the Indian language, they also established a school. The Cayuse weren't quite like any Indians they had ever heard about. A fiercely independent tribe of horsemen, they often vanished completely for weeks at a time and then reappeared without warning. When they were in the Walla Walla Valley they made themselves at home in the Whitman house, "especially at mealtime," Narcissa noted. But if they were a nuisance, they seemed to be willing converts and that, after all, was why she went west in the first place. In a year or so, the couple were reasonably settled, the school was prospering and serving the half-breed children of mountain men, who never forgot their first impression of Narcissa as she crossed the Rockies. The girls among them helped with the housework and the missionary board had provided them with a Hawaiian houseboy to help tidy up. Still, the Noble Savages Narcissa had come to save wore down her patience. "They are so filthy they make a great deal of cleaning wherever they go," she said, "and this wears a woman very fast." But if she was an overworked woman, she also remembered her Christian mission, and after mastering the Indian language she took great delight in singing hymns and reading Bible stories with them.

Doctor Whitman, meanwhile, decided that something more was needed than words and music, and concluded that the best way to lead the Indians to salvation was to teach them farming. The plain above the river was soon filled with melons and tomatoes, corn and cucumbers, blending among the buttercups and honeysuckle and other wildflowers that provided food for the soul. Mountain men often came down from the hills with news from the world beyond, and travelers of every description detoured up the Walla Walla River to share the Whitmans' hospitality. It was a rough existence, but it had its rewards, and for Narcissa one of the best of the rewards was the arrival of her daughter, Alice Clarissa.

When the child was two years old, however, she wandered into the river and drowned, and on that day, it seemed, everything changed at Waiilatpu. The Indians, who had often noted that they had been much happier back in the days when they knew of nothing more than hunting, eating, drinking and sleeping, and had no worries about the realities and responsibilities of the Christian life, began skipping Sunday services. They stopped sending their children to school, too, and though they still seemed to enjoy the vegetables from the mission farm, they began to resent the work involved in producing them. Dr. Whitman was also appalled to discover that in the four years since he arrived in the valley, no less than half the entire Indian population there had been wiped out by diseases that didn't exist in the Northwest before the white men came. And as their doctor, the survivors were beginning to blame him.

To make matters worse, Jesuit priests were arriving in the area, and to a Calvinist like Marcus Whitman the hated Catholics were the messengers of Satan himself. Of course, the leader of the movement, Father Pierre-Jean De Smet, didn't see things quite the same way. One of the most impressive missionaries in the history of Christianity, he covered some 50,000 miles in the 1840s alone, and in the process touched the lives of every Indian tribe from Minnesota to the Pacific. And even those who didn't worship his God worshipped him. Like Daniel in the lion's den, he traveled alone, living among the Indians, sharing their food and shelter and, yes, loving them. He moved from village to village, telling them stories about Jesus over their campfires, and before leaving he baptized them all. If they didn't understand the symbolism of the baptism, the ritual of the mass appealed to them and, at least for a while, they became devout Catholics. But for all his Christian principles, Father De Smet wasn't above throwing a few doubts in the path of the Protestants as he moved along. He made it a point to make sure his converts understood that the Protestant missionaries, who he called "ministers" as though it were a dirty word, weren't delivering the true Word. And in a report on the Whitman's mission, he wrote, "They cultivate a small farm large enough for their own maintenance …. It appears they are fearful that should they cultivate more they might have too frequent visits from the savages … whom they have come so far to seek." In the same report, he noted that he had baptized no less than 4,000 savages.

Dr. Whitman, of course, had no truck with baptism, and he wasted a lot of time telling the Indians that it had been a meaningless gesture. The priests had also left crosses behind, and Whitman found himself denouncing that symbol, too, as a meaningless trapping of Popery and idolatry. He told the Indians that unless they began living disciplined lives they were doomed to death and damnation. Unfortunately, he had mastered their language but never bothered to probe their psyche. The Indians may have been confused by the conflicting concepts of Christianity, but they understood that they didn't care for the one that called them sinners for doing what had always come naturally. As a result, things went from bad to worse for the Whitman mission. When the Cayuse appeared there at all, it was to challenge and ridicule the Doctor and to ride their horses through his garden. Before long, Waiilatpu was an island of rejected Protestantism surrounded on all sides by Catholics and barbarians which, to Marcus Whitman at least, were the same thing.

The situation was no better for the Spaldings, either, and when word of their troubles got back to Boston, the mission board decided to throw in the towel. Whitman responded by traveling back east to plead with them and to try to encourage more Protestants to move into the Oregon Territory and create a more favorable Catholic-Protestant balance. Almost as soon as he left, rumors spread among the Indians that he had gone to find more settlers to take their land and to bring soldiers to kill them.

When she heard the rumors, Narcissa moved to the safety of Fort Walla Walla and, over the next two years before her husband returned, lived in the relative safety of Oregon City. Her health failed during that time, but Marcus insisted that they should move back into the wilderness and continue their work.

They had their work cut out for them. The Indians were openly scornful and the whites who were settling in the valley were no help at all. When melons were stolen from his garden, a white farmer laced the rest of them with a strong laxative to teach the thieves a lesson. But the lesson received was a confirmation of the Indians' belief that white men wanted to see them suffer and die. Then, when Whitman set out poisoned meat to kill wolves and killed an Indian instead, they were convinced that they had been right. Worse, the Americans who were streaming into the valley brought measles and dysentery with them. The Cayuse had dealt with such plagues before, but now they began seeing it as a curse. The whites suffered from the same diseases but they always recovered. The Indians invariably died. The difference, as they saw it, was the medicine Dr. Whitman was giving them. Surely it wasn't medicine at all, but poison.

Their revenge was slow in coming, but swift when it arrived. On the morning of November 29, 1847, a band of Indians descended on the mission, and after murdering a tailor went into the house demanding medicine. As Whitman was handing it over, they shot him. Narcissa was upstairs, and when she was drawn to a window by the commotion, she, too, was hit by a bullet. She managed to get down to her husband, and as she was attempting to dress his wound axe-wielding Indians burst into the room and clubbed the man to death. Then they dragged her out of the house by the hair and kicked her to death. Before the day ended a half-dozen other whites were massacred, and before soldiers arrived several days later thirteen others had been killed and fifty taken hostage. Reverend Spalding was not among the victims. Ironically, he was saved by one of the hated Jesuits.

The priest had gone to Waiilatpu that day to baptize some Indian children, but when he arrived he found the mission deserted except for the mutilated bodies of the victims. After burying them, he met Spalding along the road and warned him to go into hiding, giving him a horse and provisions to make it possible. Spalding stayed out of sight for six days and was eventually saved by friendly Nez Percé Indians, but he never returned to his ministry. The Cayuse eventually surrendered a group of braves who passed for ringleaders, and after accepting a Catholic baptism they were hanged one by one.

The hangings were supposed to serve as a warning to other Indians that the white man's justice could be swift and terrible, and for a while it seemed that they had taken the message to heart. But the Whitman massacre had a profound effect on the white community, not only in the Northwest but on the other side of the country, too. It was the final straw that broke the back of any resistance to giving Washington its own territorial status and providing it with the protection of the U.S. Army. The troops arrived at Fort Vancouver a little more than a year later.

By the time they arrived along with the spring flowers in 1849 there had been dramatic changes in the West. California had become part of the United States, and Americans who had been thinking of resettling on the other side of the continent began to rethink their plans now that the Mexicans had moved out. Then, when gold was discovered in the

Sierras, the Oregon country looked even less attractive. Even Washingtonians began moving south.

But with the creation of the Washington Territory, the politicians at the Washington back east began plotting to solve the Indian "problem" there by restricting the movement of the red men and herding them together on reservations, where they wouldn't bother anybody. They made it a point to be civilized about it, and rather than ride roughshod over the Indians' rights to land they had occupied since their ancestors hunted mastodons there, they agreed among themselves that seven cents an acre might be a fair price to pay them. They wanted some two million acres, which brought the price to about $150,000. But as often happens with government plans, they couldn't spare that much cash. That was no problem, though. What were savages going to do with money anyway? It was much better, the lawmakers agreed, to pay them in "useful articles." And as another rude introduction to the ways of civilization, payment would be spread out over twenty years. The deal was described in glowing terms during a powwow of all the Western tribes called by the new governor, Isaac I. Stevens, in 1854. The Indians agreed to think about it, and from there Stevens began a tour of the Territory, visiting nearly all the tribes and getting the signatures of leaders he often designated himself on individual treaties. They varied from tribe to tribe, but the bottom line was always the same: the Indians would lose their land. It took Stevens two years to collect all the necessary signatures and another three years for Congress to ratify the treaties, and if time is supposed to heal all wounds, this time it opened an ugly one.

Stevens had been careful to explain to the chiefs that they wouldn't be required to give up their lands until the treaties were ratified, but he neglected to tell the whites the same thing. In an expanding territory like Washington that would have been a problem even under normal circumstances, but in 1855, before the ink was dry on the first of the treaties, gold was discovered along the Colville River and prospectors began rushing across the Yakima Valley. The Yakima Indians responded by killing many of them, and the new government back in Olympia reacted by sending the militia into Eastern Washington to avenge the dead miners and to take land that, by its own law, still belonged to the Yakimas. By the time the troops arrived, the Eastern tribes had united and were ready for war. And while the soldiers were in the east, the Western tribes attacked settlements near Puget Sound and even threatened Seattle. The war saw several bloody battles, but during the four years it lasted it was characterized by quick and deadly raids on farms and settlements and sudden ambushes of Indian hunting parties, the sort of thing we call terrorism today. No part of the Territory was safe from its unnerving effects, and before it ended with the Senate's final ratification of the Indian treaties, neither side had any reason to be self-righteous. There were no real heroes, no genuine villains. It was all a misunderstanding. But it cost the lives of hundreds of innocent bystanders and made thousands more think twice about making Washington their home.

But as he was dealing with the war, Governor Stevens was also preparing for peace. During his trips into the interior he busied himself making surveys for a railroad that would stretch from the Mississippi River to Seattle, where the Puget Sound would serve as a major jumping-off point for the China trade. In 1857, when he became the Territory's representative in Congress, his colleagues were at each other's throats over the issues that would soon boil over in the Civil War, but he managed to get them to agree to his plan. He told Northerners that the line would reduce the distance between New York and Shanghai by 13,000 miles, and charmed Southerners by telling them that the potential market for cotton in the Far East was equal to the entire crop they were producing at that moment.

Congressional approval almost never means instant action, but during the Civil War years it chartered three different companies to see what could be done. Each of them was given a 20-foot right-of-way, as well as other public land that could be sold to finance the construction. The Union Pacific and the Central Pacific combined their resources, and became first to cross the continent when their lines were united in Utah in 1869. But the Northern Pacific, the line Stevens had proposed, had yet to drive its first spike, and the competing railroad terminated at Sacramento, a long haul from Puget Sound.

A New York financier named Jay Cooke decided there was room for competition and, after buying the Northern Pacific's charter, lobbied Congress to change its land grant to a 120 mile-wide swath along the Columbia River and into Portland. He planned to turn north at that point, bound for Puget Sound. But to the consternation of Seattleites, Cooke decided to make Tacoma his railhead. It turned Tacoma into a boomtown, but the boom was short lived. Only a few months after announcing his decision, Cooke went bankrupt and work stopped with the N.P.'s line no further west than Bismarck, North Dakota.

But the smell of money was there, and Henry Villard, another capitalist from New York, took up the challenge. Villard already controlled the Oregon Steamship Company, and had made history when, as an enthusiastic investor in Thomas Edison's electric light, he created the first electrically-lit seagoing vessels. By 1880, he had reorganized the steamship company to include the operation of some small railroad lines, and when he heard that other entrepreneurs were planning to revive the Northern Pacific, he knew that they would swallow him up if they were successful. There was nothing to do but swallow them up first, but it would take eight million dollars to buy enough voting power on the company's board. Villard rose to the occasion by writing to fifty of his well-heeled friends asking them to invest in a scheme he had in mind. There was just one catch, he added: he couldn't tell them what the money was for until after it was spent.

Anyone who has ever gone to a bank for a personal loan might think that Villard didn't have the remotest chance of getting even polite refusals. But instead of laughing, his friends forwarded checks. And when word got around Wall Street that Henry Villard was running a blind pool, hundreds of others wrote to him begging to be allowed to jump in themselves. Making every effort to appear reluctant, Villard accepted another twelve million, which he used to finish the line between Portland and St. Paul, Minnesota. Ten years later, in 1883, Washington had its transcontinental railroad. But Seattle, which had always dreamed of being the Queen City of Puget Sound, was still on the outside looking in. The city's boosters had been arguing for nearly twenty years that Seattle was the only logical place to run a railroad to, but their pleas fell on deaf ears until a one-eyed Canadian came to town.

His name was James J. Hill, and he arrived by way of St. Paul, where he had bought a bankrupt railroad with dreams of pushing it from the

Mississippi to Puget Sound. But he wasn't like the other railroad barons. Jim Hill was a builder and frequently showed up with a pick and shovel of his own as the line, which he called "The Great Northern," pushed westward. Jim was also a promoter. When the railroad was finished, he offered ten dollar tickets to immigrants from Ellis Island in return for a promise that they'd settle along the Northern's right-of-way. He also put freight cars at their disposal to carry whatever they thought they needed, from cows to bedding, to help them get established. He used his promotional genius to build new markets for lumber from the Northwest, too, and after finding customers for them, he delighted the timber companies by cutting his freight rates.

Seattleites loved Jim Hill, and it seemed that the feeling was mutual. But nobody knew for sure whether he'd end The Great Northern there. The town of Bellingham had offered him free right-of-way and made it plain that he could have the whole town if he needed it. It made sense to people who were willing to put aside the civic pride, because Bellingham had closer access to the Strait of Juan de Fucca, the gateway to the Pacific. So did Everett. Yes, that was it. The Northern's trains were going to wind up there, they said. They were going to cross the Cascades through Skagit Pass and both Everett and Bellingham were closer to it than Seattle. But Jim Hill said nothing. When he did talk, it was almost a whisper, and the message was delivered by one of his lawyers. Even the lawyer was surprised, but it was apparent that the impression he himself had made on the railroad man was more important than any advantages the city had. Jim had met Judge Thomas Burke on an earlier visit and, after thinking it over, gave him a free hand to acquire the necessary land and to deal with the local governments. His choice proved nearly perfect, both in terms of the man and of the city. Before the project was completed, Hill was pleased to present a plan for underground tracks leading to a modern terminal, and by the time it was finished in 1905, the Northern Pacific had agreed to make the city its destination in the Northwest, too. From that moment on, there was never any more question about which city would be the Queen of Puget Sound.

It's odd that there should ever have been any question. She has one of the greatest natural harbors on the Pacific Coast; in the world, for that matter. But, though more than 18.5 million tons of shipping pass through the Port of Seattle each year, it is best known as the pleasure boat capital of America, with close to a half-million privately-owned craft, from kayaks to seagoing yachts. And though the railroads still haul freight to Seattle's piers, passenger service is largely limited to people who know that the trip across the mountains is still one of the most spectacular anywhere in the world. It doesn't matter any more that Seattle was once the greatest rail center west of Chicago. The airplane has changed everything. It changed Seattle itself. For the better.

It all dates back to the day a rich kid named Bill Boeing arrived in town. He had grown up with all the advantages: schooling in Switzerland, a generous allowance, the prospect of a huge inherited fortune from his family's interests in the rich iron mines of Minnesota. He was about to enter his final year at Yale when his father died and his mother remarried. He didn't approve of her choice and decided to leave home. New Haven wasn't far enough away from Minnesota, so he went in the opposite direction almost as far as he could go and ended up in Seattle. Young Boeing had the means to become a playboy, but he had too much energy for that. Instead, he invested his money in timber land and became a respectable member of the local business community, even though he was still a long way from thirty. He did indulge himself a bit by having a yacht custom-built, but in Seattle that was more a sign of practicality than self-indulgence, even though very few Seattleites had the means to buy the shipyard if they weren't pleased with its work, as Bill Boeing did.

He didn't know much about shipbuilding, but a fellow member of the local University Club, Conrad Westerveldt, who was an engineer at the Bremerton Navy Yard, was willing to help. But they talked about more than boats. In their conversations they discovered that each had an unfulfilled desire to take a ride in an airplane. It was only natural that when a seaplane landed in Elliott Bay they were on hand to hitch a ride. The plane was a two-seater and Boeing bravely volunteered to go first. They didn't go very high, but when they landed it was obvious that Bill Boeing's head was still in the sky, and would be there for the rest of his life. Westerveldt was smitten, too, but if Boeing was thinking about becoming a pilot, the engineer gave voice to another thought. "We could build a better airplane than this," he said. Boeing agreed and work on the yacht was forgotten.

They recruited Herb Munter, a local stunt flier who had already built a plane, and on July 15, 1916 formed the Boeing & Westerveldt Company. They built two planes at Boeing's shipyard and, while they were under construction, Boeing himself went to California to take flying lessons from the legendary Glenn Martin. When the first plane was ready, he was ready, too, and became the company's first test pilot.

When World War I broke out, they were ready for it with a plane they called the Model C, which they sold to the Navy. But when the war was over, the Navy, which didn't care much for the design anyway, cancelled its contract and B&W was stuck with what the locals were already calling The Big Kite Factory, and no potential customers other than occasional barnstormers who could afford to buy airplanes rather than build their own.

Westerveldt bowed out, but Boeing was determined to keep the company alive until enough people became interested in flying to create a demand for passenger planes. In the meantime, he decided to use his factory and the carpenters on his payroll to build furniture. They built everything from umbrella stands to phone booths to boudoir dressing tables. But when his losses began to approach $100,000, a sizeable fortune back in 1919, Boeing decided to stick to his last and get back into aviation.

Using one of the planes they had built for the Navy, he and one of his test pilots flew through a snowstorm from Seattle to Vancouver and back. They had sixty letters with them when the mission was over, the first airmail ever delivered, and Bill Boeing knew where the future was. The company's Model 40 was next off the drawing board. It was designed to carry mail, but it also had seats for passengers, even though in 1919 it was a brave American indeed who wouldn't say with firm conviction, "You'll never get me up in one of those things."

The Post Office was interested, although officials weren't eager to risk the lives of any mailmen just to speed up their service. Boeing countered by offering to fly the mail in his own planes with his own pilots on a contract basis. If the government had known that the little fleet would eventually become United Airlines, they might have handled the deal a little differently.

By the time war broke out again in Europe, Boeing was already providing the military with training planes and pursuit planes, and the Army Air Force had put the company's engineers to work designing a long-range bomber. The plane was ready in 1934, long before the U.S. got into the war, and several were already seeing service with the RAF well before 1941. But the B-17 was unknown to Americans until a week after the attack on Pearl Harbor, when it became a symbol of hope with the dramatic name "Flying Fortress." Fortress it was. It carried a crew of nine and a 10,500-lb bomb load. It had eight pairs of 0.5 caliber machine guns mounted in hydraulically-controlled turrets that pointed in every direction, and a heavy-caliber cannon in its nose. It flew about 300 miles an hour at 30,000 feet, and its range was about equal to the distance between Greenland and Britain, the delivery route followed by the ferry pilots of most of the 12,000 B-17s Boeing built. The company also designed and built the B-24 Liberator, the B-26 Marauder and the B-29 Superfortress, the plane that dropped the atomic bombs on Japan. The bombs, incidentally, used plutonium manufactured at a secret facility at Hanford in Eastern Washington. In 1952, Boeing built the first jet-age bomber, the B-47 Stratojet, which took the company into the age of jet-powered transportation with its 707 and on to the 747, the giant that made jet setters of us all, and is almost as much a source of pride to Americans as the B-17 was all those years ago.

Now that we have an airplane that can carry five hundred of us at a time, along with all our luggage, to any point in the world in less time than it takes for a flight attendant to produce change for a twenty dollar bill, it's getting harder and harder to find places where nobody has ever been. But there is a place that at least seems unexplored, and it's not very far from Seattle-Tacoma International Airport. It is Olympic National Park, a 1,431-square-mile virgin wilderness on the Olympic Peninsula between Puget Sound and the sea. Of course, there is a beaten path to it. But the roads tend to go around the park rather than through it, and there are still some mountain peaks in there that have never been climbed, much less named. The western slopes of the mountains get more moisture than any other place in the contiguous United States, an amazing 140 inches of rain and snow every year. But the northeast side of the peninsula is the driest spot on the West Coast except for the deserts of Southern California. The contrasts also include rugged seascapes with seals basking in the sun and jagged mountains that are home to some 5,000 elk. The mountains rise up abruptly from sea level to 5,000 feet and more, all the way up to the nearly 8,000-foot Mount Olympus. But there are mountains and seacoasts in other places, too. What make this place unique is the rainforests of the western valleys. All that moisture brings a special reward in the form of dense forests of Sitka spruce, western hemlock, Douglas fir and Western red cedar growing out of a deep, spongy blanket of moss that clings to the tree trunks and hangs down like cobwebs from the lower branches. Even on bright days not much light penetrates to the forest floor, and there are few places in the world where civilization and jumbo jets seem so far away.

The peninsula was one of the last places on the American continent to be explored. Washington was already celebrating statehood when the mountains were crossed for the first time, and it has only been one hundred years since an expedition was sent in to probe their mysteries. Not even the Indians ever went up into those mountains. Their legends told them that a giant bird lived up there in the snow, and that any man who approached even the lowest slopes would be torn apart by its talons. Besides, there were plenty of fish in the sea and oysters on the beach and game was abundant on the coastal plain, and there was no reason take a chance that the legend might not be true. The earliest settlers weren't frightened by Indian legends, but they didn't have any reason to explore the interior, either. It wasn't that they weren't curious about it, though. It was plain to everyone that the mountain peaks seemed to form a triangle, and that, naturally, led to speculation about what was in the middle. Nearly everyone agreed that the three mountain walls enclosed a great plain. None of them believed in the Indian tales of a big bird, but they weren't above fantasizing on their own, and many were sure that the hidden valley was the home of a race of fierce cannibals. Some were just as convinced that there must be gold and silver there, but few of them were brave enough to go in and find out.

That job was left to the Army. In 1885, an expedition led by Lt. Joseph P. O'Neil penetrated the wilderness south of Port Angeles, but not long after they arrived in the high country the Army, in its wisdom, transferred O'Neil to Kansas, sending a messenger all the way to the base camp on Mount Anderson to deliver the orders. But the Lieutenant went back to Washington five years later and picked up where he left off, exploring and mapping the peninsula. When he and his men got back to civilization, they were happy to report that there were no man-eating birds or man-eating people up there, and though they hadn't found any evidence of vast mineral deposits, O'Neil was enthusiastic about the huge stands of timber he had found, and though he noted the supply wasn't inexhaustible, he said that the land the loggers cleared would be perfect for farming. But he was talking about the land south and west of the mountains. He reported that the most of the region was "absolutely unfit for any use," and suggested that it probably would make a nice national park. People nodded in agreement, and then promptly forgot all about O'Neil and his advice. Prospectors tramped through the foothills and came out empty-handed. Nature reclaimed the trails the O'Neil party had cut, and though the government created a forest reserve there in 1897, a proposal to create "Elk National Park" was voted down in 1904. Five years later, President Theodore Roosevelt enthusiastically created the Mount Olympus National Monument, but in another ten years timber and mining lobbyists managed to have the Monument reduced to half its size. Another President Roosevelt elevated it to national park status in 1938, and two years later he increased its size to what had been intended in the first place. It had been fifty years since O'Neil and his men went up into the mountains, but the place hadn't changed a bit. It still hasn't.

There are glaciers and spectacular waterfalls, magnificent rivers and breathtaking mountains on the peninsula, but what makes the Olympics, and all of Washington, for that matter, so special are the trees. In the area just inland from Gray's Harbor, the Douglas firs were so thick that for more than thirty years they could only be cut in one direction, and because the forest was so dense, there wasn't any room to cut them into logs. But if loggers and nature lovers are impressed by these giants, their enthusiasm doesn't hold a candle to David Douglas, the man who gave the tree its name.

Douglas arrived on the banks of the Columbia in 1824 on a mission for England's Royal Horticultural Society, to find new plants and trees that could be grown back home. The ship that took him there was scheduled to pick him up in six months, and by the time it did he had collected five hundred likely specimens. But it wasn't an easy job. Because of the rain and the damp moss that was as much as six inches thick, it was hard for him to dry out the specimens he gathered, but it had to be done or they would die and become useless. When he got beyond the mountains, the hot sun dried out the plants and seeds too fast, but Douglas muddled through. He was an enthusiastic little man, and though he traveled alone, he was given to shouts of glee when he ran across a new plant. The Indians thought he was quite strange, but they also noticed that he was handy with a rifle and decided it was best to indulge his peculiarities. When he wasn't searching the ground for wildflowers and grasses, he was looking above his head at the magnificent trees. He identified the Western white pine, the ponderosa pine, the silver fir and dozens of other varieties. He admired the tree that would eventually bear his name, but didn't give it the name. That would come later when the honor would be bestowed by his sponsors, who didn't realize the tree isn't a fir at all, but a close cousin of the hemlock. Douglas was excited by the tree's size, but he hadn't seen anything anything yet.

The Indians were eager to help, even though they couldn't figure out what he was doing, and one day some of them offered to share some nuts they had gathered. But what they produced wasn't a nut at all. It was a pine cone. But the botanist had never seen one so big. The red men told him that they grew far away to the south, but they warned him that he shouldn't go there because it was a land filled with evil spirits. Trappers told him it was a land of endless rain, but Douglas was determined to see this tree for himself and, throwing caution to the winds, headed south. The trees he found there were well over two hundred feet high and measured fifty seven feet around. And their lowest branches were more than a hundred feet above his head. The pine cones hanging there were as much as two feet long. But there was a problem. There was no way to get at them, and a botanist without samples is no better than a sightseer. He decided to shoot one down with his pistol, and his aim was good enough to get a big cone with one bullet. But the sound attracted an Indian hunting party who, unlike their northern neighbors, didn't find the botanist cute. Douglas tried smiling and making friendly gestures, but just got grim stares in response. Then he tried a different approach. He aimed his rifle at the leader's chest and waved his pistol in the general direction of the others. They finally backed off and began smiling themselves. They'd let him go, they said, if the white man would give them tobacco. But David Douglas was from Scotland. He wanted more for his money. He told them he'd give them the tobacco if they'd get him more of those giant pine cones to take with him when they let him go. It must have been the glint in his eye that convinced them, because they gathered more than he could possibly carry. They probably wondered for the rest of their lives what in the world he planned to do with them.

What he planned, of course, was to tell the world about this wonderful tree he had discovered. It was the Western sugar pine, far and away the biggest member of its family and the tree Douglas considered the greatest find of his career. He carried the cones back up to the Columbia and arrived in time to make the rendezvous with his ship. But, after packing up his specimens for transport back to England, he told the captain that, though he appreciated the offer of a ride, he'd rather walk, and set off on a specimen-collecting hike across Canada.

By the time Douglas got back to England, his samples had already arrived and he was a famous man. But more famous still were the forests of the Northwest, which he had proven once and for all weren't the figment of anybody's imagination. And though men have been hacking away at them with axes and saws ever since, they still have to be seen to be believed. Even though the lumber companies are producing more than five billion board feet each and every year, there are still well over twenty-three million acres of uncut forests in the State of Washington, covering an area quite a bit larger than the entire Pine Tree State of Maine. But then, the Evergreen State of Washington is bigger than all the New England states combined.

But this place that was once called Nova Albion isn't at all like New England. It isn't like any other place on the continent, in fact. Ask a group of Washingtonians to describe the place, and you'll probably end up confused. They might describe cattle ranches or fog-bound fishing towns, endless fields of wheat or tidy orchards heavy with juicy apples. They might talk about salmon leaping over waterfalls or magnificent elk at sunrise on the shore of a crystal clear lake. They could be city people, too, or they might commute to jobs in the city from homes on otherwise deserted islands. But whatever they find to like about life in Washington, they all agree that there is nothing quite like it. And who's to say they aren't absolutely right?

Previous page: Old Glory flies beside the apex of the U.S. Pavilion in Spokane's Riverfront Park (right), the centerpiece of this eastern Washington city. The park was built for the 1974 World's Fair Expo and replaced disused railroad tracks, yards and stations with a theater, an ice rink and a children's zoo, as well as an opera house and a convention center. Spokane is the second largest city in the state and the largest between Seattle and Minneapolis. It was the site of the state's first trading post, established in 1810, though permanent settlement didn't begin until 1871. Overleaf: morning light silvers the summit of Mount Adams, whose perfect reflection appears in Takhlakh Lake in the Mount Adams Wilderness, southern Washington.

Left: a great cauldron of dark water receives Palouse Falls, the highlight of Palouse Falls State Park where Eastern Washington's Palouse River winds through dramatically eroded canyons (above) and sage-brush covered hills on its way to join the Snake River. The park, which lies north of the small town of Starbuck, boasts ten campsites and an excellent view of the 190-foot-high falls.

Above: Union Pacific locomotives traverse a steel bridge near Lyon's Ferry State Park. In the late nineteenth century the railroads provided the means by which loggers could get their timber to market – and, indeed, one railroad, the Northern Pacific, went so far as to sell its government-granted land to logging operations, knowing that it would be able to reap huge profits as the sole means of transport for such concerns. Above right: the McNary Dam and its fish ladder, which allows fish to negotiate this stretch of the Columbia River beside the Horse Heaven Hills. Right and overleaf: Grand Coulee Dam, the world's greatest producer of hydroelectrical power. This dam in central Washington is nearly a mile long and twice as high as Niagara Falls. Using the Columbia River, it supplies energy to several states and irrigates half a million acres of farmland.

These pages: velvety folds of Palouse farmland in Eastern Washington. The Palouse is a region that stretches over 4,000 square miles and includes part of Idaho as well as Washington. It is exceptionally fertile land, where the topsoil, even on the brows of many hills, can be over four feet in depth. Harvesting wheat on such steep hills was once a dangerous business, since ordinary combines risk toppling on the gradients, but in the thirties a self-leveling machine was invented and the Palouse has never looked back. Nevertheless, tilling methods have ground the soil into tiny particles which can be eroded from the hills to the tune of 300 tons per acre on occasions, a serious danger which Palouse farmers need to employ careful land management to avoid.

Right and overleaf: agriculture in Whitman County in the Palouse region. This county has averaged forty bushels of wheat per acre since 1934, compared to the average U.S. yield of twenty bushels – fertility is not a problem here! The word Palouse is thought to have originated from the French for lawn, pelouse, *which was what trappers nicknamed the region when they came across so much bunchgrass there. Today such land is cherished by a farming community whose members are reluctant to retire – it is estimated that over sixty percent of them are over fifty; many still farm at seventy.*

A harvested wheatfield in Yakima County, central southern Washington, which is covered in a volcanic soil that is twice as productive as ordinary land. Such soil, coupled with a climate that provides an average of 300 sunny days per year and irrigation schemes that make good use of the Yakima River, ensures that Yakima produces more apples, hops and mint than any other county in the entire United States. Cattle men were the first to settle the region as farmers initially condemned the soil as too dry to be productive. The first irrigation ditch was dug in the 1860s, after which the true wealth of the soil was revealed – farmers today see the Yakima Valley as a latter day Garden of Eden, claiming that it is possible to grow anything here.

Above: serene blue skies stretch over the Staton Hills winery and vineyard in the Yakima Valley. This valley is famous for its wineries, most of which can be found strung along the Yakima River southeast of Yakima city. The Yakima and Columbia valleys combined are the state's major wine-growing regions, and vineyard owners are quick to point out that these districts are on the same latitude as the renowned Burgundy and Bordeaux regions of France. Indeed, the wine produced in Yakima Valley is some of the finest in the Northwest. Left: bullocks and bullrushes in countryside around Ellensburg, a quiet town of some 12,000 souls known for its Labor Day rodeo which attracts spectators and participators from across the land. Overleaf: a wooden barn on rangeland in the central Cascades Range.

On May 18 1980 at 8.31 in the morning, Mount St. Helens, the youngest volcanic mountain in the Cascades Range, exploded. The blast was loud enough to be heard in Vancouver, some 200 miles to the north, its force being 500 times more powerful than that of the atomic bomb dropped on Hiroshima. Over 150 square miles of timber were flattened and the popular recreational area of Spirit Lake (above) was devastated by hurricane winds and tons of volcanic ash. Once a beautifully symmetrical mountain (facing page), today Mount St. Helens is only two-thirds of its former size with a broad, flattened summit. In the past decade hiking trails have been cleared and now it is even possible to climb the mountain and travel across the crater floor. Since volcanic ash is potentially extremely fertile, the devastated area will recover. Lushness such as can still be found in parts of Gifford Pinchot National Forest (overleaf), much of which was affected by the eruption, will one day be as common in the region as it was before that fateful day in May.

A lupin meadow forms an inviting foreground to Mount Rainier, the sleeping volcano that is the highest peak in the Cascade mountain range. The mountain is the centerpiece of Mount Rainier National Park, a scenic wilderness sixty miles southeast of Tacoma that is visited by over one-and-a-half million people annually. The mountain was named by the explorer Captain George Vancouver for a friend, one Rear Admiral Peter Rainier, who never actually saw the 14,411-high summit. Such a great height means that the mountain has a dramatic effect on the weather by interrupting the air flow around it; this leads to world-record levels of snowfall on its slopes. Overleaf: a perfect reflection of Mount Rainier in Reflection Lake.

Above: a waterfall along a hiking trail in Mount Rainier National Park. Falls such as Christine Falls (facing page), where Van Trump Creek splashes down a black rock face, are one of the reasons the trails in this park are so popular: the Wonderland Trail for backpackers is one of the best known: it comprises ninety-three miles of mountain passes, forests and alpine meadows that completely encircle the mountain. Although the season for such treks is short – the mountain is only snow-free from mid-July to mid-October – sights such as meadows full of wild lupins (overleaf) near Sunrise, a visitor center north of the mountain, make them worth taking.

Left: the Grove of the Patriarchs, Mount Rainier National Park. The name of this clearing is a reference to the magnificent Douglas firs present here, which can reach heights of over three hundred feet with a diameter of more than ten. This tree is not mature until it is between two and three hundred years old and it is estimated that some Douglas firs are still viable at 1,000 years of age. Above: the Hall of Mosses in Olympic National Park on the Pacific coast. This park receives the greatest precipitation of any spot in the conterminous United States and such a profusion of mosses, lichen and fungi are the result in some of the most luxuriant rain forests in the world.

Right: lilies of the field bloom in startling profusion on the slopes of Mount Rainier in spring, when even the bogs bloom (overleaf). These wildflowers bloom progressively higher up the mountain as the summer passes, so that in effect the mountain experiences only two seasons – winter and spring. Mount Rainier National Park was created in 1899 to preserve the beauty of the Cascades, especially the exceptional kingdom of glaciers to be found on Mount Rainier's slopes – the mountain's glacier system is recognized as the most extensive "single peak" glacial system in the country outside Alaska; there are forty-one rivers of ice to be found on these slopes, one of which is the longest in the conterminous U.S., and another of which, the Emmons Glacier, is the largest.

The town of Winthrop lies in Okanogan County in northern Washington, just outside the North Cascades National Park on the North Cascades Highway. Before the completion of this highway, the town was less than prosperous, but since it has gained a new lease on life, having decided to construct wooden sidewalks and false-front stores all along its Main Street (these pages) that are reminiscent of the town's colorful mining days during the last century. These features serve to attract visitors on their way to the park and such attention from travelers has meant that Winthrop has become the commerical center of the Methrow Valley area.

The northern part of Lake Chelan, a long, thin glacial lake, is the centerpiece of Lake Chelan National Recreation Area, close to Northern Cascades National Park. The lake resembles a fjord, being over a mile wide, fifty-five miles long and 1,500 feet deep; indeed it is one of the deepest inland stretches of water in the world. The recreation area around it was established by Congress with the specific prohibition of the construction of roads from the outside world to the Stehekin Valley, an isolated, extremely beautiful area at the head of the lake. The little town of Stehekin can only be reached by boat, seaplane or on foot. Set amid superb mountain scenery, the area is still relatively unknown and, as a consequence, its natural, unspoilt state has been preserved.

These pages and overleaf: Leavenworth overflows
with colorful windowbox blooms in high
summer. In the early sixties, in a move similar to
that made in Winthrop, the people of
Leavenworth made a conscious decision to re-
design their main buildings and, with the
support of the local banks, they created an Alpine
look-alike. Now shops, restaurants, taverns and
hotels are all sporting carved wood, sloping roofs,
white paint and black exterior timber decoration,
and Leavenworth is known all over the state as
the Bavarian Village. With its mountainous
position adding to the illusion and its numerous
festivals providing varied entertainment,
Leavenworth has become one of the most popular
year-round resorts in the Cascades.

Over 9,000 feet high, Mount Shuksan (these pages and overleaf) looms over aptly named Picture Lake in North Cascades National Park. Shuksan lies in the northern part of the park in the Picket Range, close to the Canadian border, and is dwarfed by nearby Mount Baker, which soars to nearly 11,000 feet. Both mountains can be viewed from picnic areas that are justifiably popular since they afford stunning views of the summits on clear days. The Heather Meadows that lie between the two peaks, and the lakes and rock formations that surround them, were the setting for the films Call of the Wild and The Deer Hunter.

Above: the jewel-like, glacier-fed waters of Diablo Lake, which is given its turquoise hue from minerals suspended in the glacial run-off. The lake lies in the center of North Cascades National Park and covers over 900 acres; it was formed by the Skagit River Hydroelectric Project designed to provide Seattle with power. Comprised largely of massive granite peaks (facing page), such as Liberty Bell and Early Winter Spires (overleaf), North Cascades National Park is Washington's third great national park and the last to be established; it was created in 1968. More than 350 miles of hiking and horse trails exist throughout the park, and backpacking and mountaineering are two of the most popular pastimes: indeed, some of the finest mountaineering opportunities in the country are to be found here.

Above and overleaf: the richest of reds in tulip fields in the Skagit River Valley. A thick growth of cedar once cloaked this valley, but that has now been replaced with fertile farms. Facing page: an antiques shop in Snohomish, a town that claims to be the antiques capital of the Pacific Northwest since it can boast over 100 antiques dealers in a four-block area. Snohomish lies to the north of Seattle and is sustained by dairy farming and the Boeing 747 plant nearby.

These pages: some examples of Port Townsend's famous Victorian architecture, the legacy of wealthy merchants of the 1880s. This collection of authentic mansions and public buildings is the best to be found north of San Francisco. Born from the town's prosperity as a busy seaport, these houses now contribute towards the town's wealth, since they are a considerable tourist attraction – as is the fact that the film An Officer and a Gentleman *was filmed here. Overleaf: La Conner, which lies on the Swinomish Channel in sight of Mount Baker. A small, historic fishing port, La Conner attracts many tourists during its spectacular Tulip Festival in the spring: the town is surrounded by bulb fields.*

Seattle's Space Needle (these pages) is undoubtedly the city's best known structure – at 520 feet in height it remains the tallest man-made object (overleaf) for miles around. The Needle is part of the Seattle Center, where a huge variety of interests can be catered for – the Center is home to theater companies, a three-tier shopping and eating emporium, the Seattle Children's Museum, an amusement park, the Opera House and the Pacific Science Center complex.

Seattle is justifiably proud of the recreational facilities on offer at its waterfront (left and overleaf). Since most industrial shipping has ceased now, the piers that were once the destination of busy cargo vessels have been given over to pedestrian-orientated pursuits, the highlight of which must be Waterfront Park. This is an area that extends from piers 57 to 59, a park without grass, but one which provides numerous picnic areas, gift shops and three waterfront streetcars for transport, as well as the Seattle Marine Aquarium and the Omnidome. In the latter an 180° dome screen presents films of erupting volcanoes, voyages in outer space and underwater excursions.

Facing page: Seattle's elegant Space Needle, designed by a Seattle architect, Victor Steinbrueck, for the 1962 World Fair. The tower is crowned by a revolving restaurant and a 360° observation deck, which offers the finest view of the surrounding cityscape and mountains beyond to be had anywhere. Above: serried ranks of yachts line Seattle's Shilshole Marina, which lies to the north of the city in Puget Sound. Close by a canal connects the waters of the Sound with Seattle's freshwater Lake Union. Overleaf: Pier 56, part of Seattle's Waterfront Park and often the visitor's first port of call, since a superb view of the harbor is available from here.

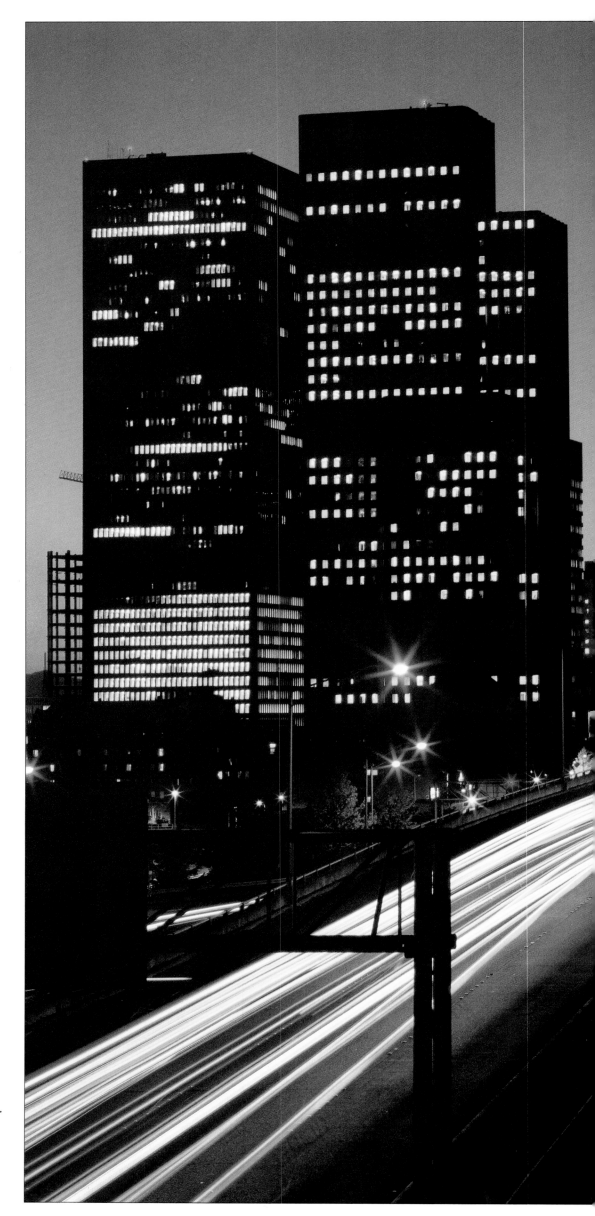

Seattle (right and overleaf) enjoys an enviable reputation as one of the nation's most desirable locations. Situated beside Puget Sound in the north of the state and backed by the majestic Cascade Range, Seattle has experienced phenomenal growth in the last half of this century. Much of this is due to the success of the nearby Boeing aircraft plant, which employs many thousands and forms the main industry in the region, but Seattle's reputation for clean air, friendly people, beautiful surroundings and justifiable civic pride is a considerable draw as well. Although a city of outdoor enthusiasts, a generally moist climate has encouraged Seattle's citizens to become strong supporters of opera, theater and cinema; the Emerald City can claim to be the cultural center of the Pacific Northwest.

Immaculate lawns and profuse spring blossoms surround the Legislative Building in Olympia. This impressive stone structure was finished in 1928, having taken over thirty years to complete. Its 287-foot dome has perfect acoustics and affords those willing to climb up to its heights spectacular views of Mount Rainier and Mount St. Helens. Olympia, the state capital, lies at the southern end of Puget Sound where pioneers first settled in the 1840s, attracted by the commercial possibilities of Deschutes Falls. Today the capital is known throughout the state as a beer-brewing center.

Above: the picturesque harbor at Tokeland, a town on the Washington coast established in the nineteenth century and named after a local Indian chief. The Shoalwater Indians, who lived on the strip of land nearby known as Toke Point, were wiped out, like so many small tribes, by smallpox carried to the region by white settlers. Tokeland is largely unspoilt and retains a nineteenth-century atmosphere. Above right: South Bend oyster shells – the mill town of South Bend on Willapa Bay boasts a fully automated oyster-processing plant. Willapa (right) is its sister town, equally involved in the oyster trade, while to the south, the Pacific town of Ilwaco (overleaf) is devoted to sea fishing, receiving many seasonal visitors eager to catch halibut, tuna and sturgeon.

Above left: romping in the waves in Grayland Beach State Park south of Westport. Above and left: driftwood on silken sands at Kalaloch and (overleaf) at La Push, both part of the coastal Olympic National Park and considered two of the last wilderness ocean beaches in the conterminous United States. This national park is among the 100 parks in the world named a "World Heritage Park" by the United Nations in 1981 for the diversity of its climate, ecology and geography. It contains primeval rain forests, eight wildflower species unique to the park, five world-record-sized trees and the country's largest population of Roosevelt elk. In such a sensitive environment, cars have been limited to the outskirts of the park to preserve its fragile interior.

Above and overleaf: the Hall of Mosses, part of the Hoh Valley rain forest that lies close to the Hoh River and one of the highlights of Olympic National Park. The western-facing valleys of the park's Bogachiel, Queets, Hoh and Quinault rivers receive between 150 and 200 inches of rain per year. Such precipitation, coupled with the warm air of the Japanese Current, encourages club moss to cover the trunks and branches of towering spruce and hemlock. Facing page: Lake Crescent, which lies in the south of the park and is locally famous for its excellent stock of Beardslee trout.

Above: wave- and wind-swept driftwood on Rialto Beach (above right), a fine storm-watching spot in the Pacific Coast area of Olympic National Park. These beaches are superb for beachcombing and tide pools remain full of sea life, while not only seabirds and sealions visit the shore – bears, elk and wildcats have been known to wander here. Right, overleaf and following page: sunsets on the Great Bend, the southernmost point of Hood Canal, which borders the Olympic Peninsula.

INDEX

Gifford Pinchot National Forest 54, 55
Grand Coulee Dam 37-39
Hood Canal 126-128
Ilwaco 114, 115
La Conner 92, 93
Lake Chelan National Recreational Area 72, 73
Leavenworth 74-77
McNary Dam 37
Mount Adams 32, 33
Mount Rainier National Park 56-64, 66-69
    Christine Falls 61
    Grove of the Patriarchs 64
    Mount Rainier 56-59, 62, 63, 66, 67
    Reflection Lake 58, 59
    Van Trump Creek 61
Mount St. Helens 53
North Cascades National Park 79-85
    Diablo Lake 82
    Early Winter Spires 84, 85
    Liberty Bell 84, 85
    Mount Shuksan 79-81
    Picture Lake 79-81
Olympia Legislative Building 110, 111
Olympic National Park 64, 65, 116-128
    Hall of Mosses 64, 65, 120, 122, 123

Kalaloch Beach 116, 117
Lake Crescent 121
La Push Beach 118, 119
Rialto Beach 124, 125
Palouse 34, 35, 40-45
    Palouse Falls 34
    Palouse River 35
    Whitman County 42-45
Port Townsend 90, 91
Seattle 94-109
    Pier 56 104, 105
    Space Needle 94, 95, 102
    Shilshole Marina 103
    Waterfront Park 98, 99, 104, 105
Skagit River Valley 86, 88, 89
Snohomish 87
South Bend 113
Spirit Lake 52
Spokane Riverfront Park 29-31
Takhlakh Lake 32, 33
Tokeland 112, 113
Willapa 113
Winthrop 70, 71
Yakima County 46, 47
    Staton Hills winery 48, 49